1

Everything you need to know
relationship is right here.

Table of Contents

Introduction

My name is Davie Sandridge. I was born and raised in Coldwater, MS, a place from where so many brilliant and skilled people came, and many are still there. I was born into a huge family of entrepreneurs, so I was able to take on a different mindset about running things for yourself and not depending on anyone else to do it for you. I grew up with both parents and a little sister, so you can say I had the old-fashioned TV family. I can't say everything was good or bad. I have just been taught to play the card you are dealt and don't complain. Do it right the first time, and you won't have to do it again. I graduated from high school and from the best HBCU, Tougaloo College, where I had the time of my life. There I received my B.A. in economics with the emphasis in business and an associate's degree in art and hotel and hospitality management Along with that, I joined the mighty brothers of Omega Psi Phi Inc., the mother chapter of MS, the Mighty Woody Rho.

I managed McDonald's for a year but got tired of getting cussed at about that damn ice cream machine, so I moved on to get my CDL. I played around with transportation and ran a business for two years. I sold cars during tax season, which was lovely because I could sell them in the winter and pick them up in the summer for auction when the owners could no longer afford them. I'm married with two children out of wedlock but with same mom. They are priority number 1.

I'm not perfect nor claim to be. I have always been a hustler and kept to a small group. I've never been a "yes" man. I always had my own way of thinking. I have always been a fan of just listening to people and learning. Helping people and making people smile is all I strive to do in life, and I take life for what it is.

The reason for this book to inspire the ain't-shit bitches and niggas in the world to stop the madness. These misguided and undecided people are some lost souls that don't have that person to give them a blueprint on how life is going to come at their ass full speed or let them know that there are decisions that have will be made that can alter their lives if they're not careful. I hope to help people see value in themselves rather than depend on someone else, or even social media, to tell them who they are and how to live because, these days, people will make you feel as if your happiness doesn't mean shit if they don't have anything to gain from it. I want to help people stop trying to get validation from these bitch ass niggas who are not even qualified to direct them.

A lot of men and women are experimenting in relationships. Stay-at-home or not-at-home niggas are on the rise. We have niggas moving in with the women or we have these silly, too independent bitches who don't want to listen or feel they don't have to listen because they feel as if they don't need a man to provide, protect, or lead them. These niggas today don't have any nuts because they feel they're not valued. Most women think that, because they run shit at work, they can run shit at home, which you do, but you can't bring work home acting as if he is your student, even if he is acting like it. Why be with him is the question you should ask yourself if he is acting like it. Leave that work shit at work, which goes for both parties.

Niggas keep letting the same bitch lock him up and keep going back to her. Bitch letting these bitch ass niggas run these sorry ass games, making it harder for real men to come into their lives because they've been abused mentally and physically by these fuck niggas.

The world is so sensitive and quick to get in their feelings which is causing the world to lose its fucking mind because there is no foundation in these young grasshoppers. Everyone follows the crowd instead of questioning the crowd. I've learned and I am still a student of all shapes of life about all the ups and downs that life has to offer. I only plan to help someone else. These experiences that I have had made my life easier but were still a round by round fight for me, so maybe I can be that brother to help others understand how to deal with these bitch ass niggas.

At the very least, I hope to help them understand why their lives may seems to be fucked up, and they just walk around blaming people for their fucked-up decisions. Nobody is perfect, but nobody should be left without just because they didn't have someone to look out for them. So, I am giving them a care package to take along with them in life that may can help.

Warning: Before You Read

Before you read this book, please remember that everybody is entitled to his or her own opinion, and that there is a reason we have freedom of speech. People get emotional so quickly, start judging and pointing a finger, not giving the time to understand a situation. We need to stop letting our emotions cloud our judgments, which mostly steer us in the wrong direction. With that being said, put your big girl and big boy drawers on. A lot of shit in this book may make your breast sweat, make you scratch your head, or say *ooohhhhh, that's right*. That means the shoes fit: now wear them, and let's take this walk and talk together. The truth sometimes hurts and medicine hardly ever tastes good. It will be a lot of things said that is not for kids, but necessary for BANs that keep producing the little-ain't-shit-motherfuckers that are going to take over the world.

Get out of your feelings and put them in your pocket while reading this book. BANs are destroying our families, relationships, and hell, the world. BANs, which is really just about an attitude, must be banned. We should start curing these BANs before we all are infected. If we sit around shit every day, pretty soon we can't smell it. BANs don't have an age or gender, just a certain type of attitude and view of life. It is never too late to stop being a bitch. I, Davie Brandon Sandridge, was once, and still am, a recovering BAN. It is something you have to fight every day because they're recruiting like the army, growing like weeds, or a fungus. I have lived as a known BAN and studied BANs throughout my life's journey. I think I may have a solution/cure for this BAN situation that is occurring among us.

Bitch is a word that is being used on a daily basis by women and men. We use it as a term of endearment, insult, or just trying to get a point across. It is all about the point of view or the situation it is being used in. In this book, a bitch is a person who is belligerent, unreasonable, and malicious, who is a control freak, rudely intrusive or aggressive. A bitch normally acts as if there are no consequences to their action, or doesn't care if there are.

Niggas are everywhere. There are many types of niggas. The select group of niggas that will be talked about in this book are the ones who steal-your-money-and-pretend-to-help-you-find-it type. At-home-with-mom-but-don't-have-a-car. A nigga who has every pair of Jordans but begging for a ride. A nigga who knows everything but never been 30 miles outside their address. A nigga who wear fake shit but trying to pass it off as the real deal. He's always asking for a smoke or buying loose cigarettes. A nigga who wants somebody to support him and his habits. A nigga who doesn't have a checking account with at least five hundred in it but claiming he is balling and making moves. It's about the niggas who just don't want to do right.

BAN Defined:

A Bitch Ass Nigga (BAN) is a person who acts as if there are no consequences to his/her actions. They don't have a cap on the level of bullshit they are willing to do or sink to, to get what they want, the way that they want it. They do not care about anyone else's feelings so are not messed up about using and manipulating those feelings to get their way with as little effort on their part as they can get away with. They are lazy and trifling and believe that everything wrong in their life is someone else's fault. They believe the world owes them everything but don't think that they have to do anything to earn what they want. They will use you, even abuse you, as long as it benefits them; and then when they are finished using you, they will just move on to the next victim. And just so you know, a BAN has no specific gender. A woman can be a BAN just as well as a man.

Lack of Direction

The leading cause of this Bitch Ass Nigga syndrome is due to the lack of direction in this world. When dealt a hand of cards, the BAN has no idea which way he should play them. Not having any direction growing up can really mess you up mentally. This is not saying you can't bounce back. It just may make it much harder. Do you know the old saying *if you know better, you do better*? Hopefully, something said in this book will help you to both know better and do better. It's all about the cards being dealt to you and how you play them. Even a bad hand can win the game…if you know what you're doing.

Most people don't grow up with the perfect family and will never have the perfect family. By perfect family, I mean the societal definition of both parents married with children. This does not include having multiple baby mamas that you're sexing because you both need somewhere to stay. You have all the benefits of a spouse with no ring or paperwork to back that shit up. Even if you were brought up in a so-called "perfect family," it doesn't guarantee you direction because the other person may have been raised by bitch ass niggas as well. The shit may just run in the family: don't let "my dad or no one was there" be an excuse. You just need to understand that you are here with a gift that the world is waiting on you to give it. Be the example of what you wanted your mom or dad to be to your kids and enjoy life. Many successful people come from a broken home, but that is no reason to use this as an excuse not to be your best or at least be better than what you know, and there is no need to keep having children if you're not going to take care of them, both emotionally and physically.

Having both parents involved in your life seems to give a person some type of foundation. You see how good chemistry between a man and woman in person works. Seeing it in person shows you a blueprint to what a relationship should be like. You get the chance to understand the give and take that a relationship needs to be stable and strong. If you are cooking, understand that when you don't know the right ingredients to use to make a particular sauce, it will never come out right regardless of what you put in it. When you don't know how to make this life thing work for you, you start to experiment and then get frustrated when things don't work out right. You can sometimes let yourself go to the point of no return if you don't catch yourselves.

The love so many people are showing now is crazy and misguided. These people are living life acting as if other people don't have feelings and wondering why they find themselves in a revolving door of bad luck. If it is a revolving door of foolishness going on for you, I strongly advise you to check yourself because you keep stepping in it. Having direction boosts the chances of success tremendously in a relationship and in the way you live life period. Directions are the layout to whatever you are trying to achieve or wherever you are trying to go. They also help with whatever you may run into during your life's journey.

Life is a journey full of choices. Some will be easy, and some will be hard; but before you make them, always think about the consequences of your actions and see how they stack up against the decisions you make. And remember, refusing to make a decision is actually still making a decision. The only difference is that, when you refuse to make the decision yourself, you open the door for someone else to make the decision for you. The choice then is simple: you can live life letting other people make your decisions for you or you can make them yourself. Have your own backbone. Have an opinion. Live for yourself and be responsible for what you create.

In life, there is always more than one way of getting things done. The best way to bob and weave through life is to get advice from other people who have been down the road you are on or who are on the road you are trying to go down. Remember, there is no one you cannot learn from. Even the worst person you know can teach you something, even if that something is just how not to act or do something.

Never let someone rob you of your time and you don't gain anything from it. Time is all we have, and it must be managed wisely. We give the job eight plus hours a day, sleep eight, and never use the other eight to build self. Don't say you are tired, because you stay putting in overtime on social media, and then, at the job that will lay your ass off if you're late or call in sick, you play around. That is why you must work on yourself—to increase your value. Master at least one thing and stop being a jack of all trades. I found that taking the time to invest in and master one thing at a time changed my life. It gave me a purpose, and now everything I do has a meaning. If it doesn't have anything to do with what I'm mastering, then I don't mess with it. If you don't value you, who will? I was told that people will come from all over the world to see you if you are valuable enough, so I spend at least thirty minutes a day every day building myself, no matter what.

Never overlook an opportunity to learn from anyone, because the person you are looking at crazy now may know something that could come at you later in life. Your mom or dad probably cannot tell you what drugs do to you, but a crackhead can. Crackheads can show you how having a lack of direction in life can lead you down a path of destruction.

Today, some people take advice and just wipe their ass with it. Advice can be vital and it is important. Advice should be thought of like tools that can help you on your journey in life. Some of the tools will be very useful right then, some just need to be tossed aside, and still others need to be locked up to be used at a later time. Are all tools good? No, but the bad ones are also good to keep in your memory bank because they still serve a purpose. They show you what not to do, and that can be just as important as what you should do.

When taking in information, it is a great idea not only to listen but to look at what the person is doing and not just telling you. Always pay attention to the details. With the technology available and the fast pace at which the world is moving, a nigga can make you think he owns the world and the whole time he's homeless. It can be a cold game and you have to be ready to play or your ass is done, because bitches today are only out for themselves and will use your ass to get what they want regardless if it hurts you or not.

Every time you come in contact with somebody, they should teach you something for taking up your time. Whatever knowledge a person is feeding you, eat it up. You should be hungry for it. Never put a cap on your wisdom. Life comes at you many different ways, and it will destroy you if you let it, so it is mandatory that you suck up all the knowledge and wisdom that comes in your life. Process that shit and learn from each situation in life. It is stupid as fuck to keep doing the same shit over and over and expecting different results. Don't be a can't-get-right person. Instead, use your strengths and wits to get things done the right way.

Everyone does not process information the same. For some people, it takes getting some bumps and bruises on them to tune that ass up. Some people can use other people's life choices to learn from just in case they are faced with some of the same bullshit moments life can bring.

No one has walked on this earth before whose shit doesn't stink, so get that perfect shit out of your head.

In this journey of life, don't underestimate the power of choices and how they can affect your body, mind, and others around you.

You have the power to see things as good or bad: it is all about how you look at the situation and the wisdom you have to see it with. You can be driving too close to a big truck, and all of a sudden, a rock smacks the shit out of your windshield giving you two choices: be a bitch and complain about ignoring the "stay back 100 feet" sign which your impatient ass clearly ignored, or learn to take your time and fall your ass back, because you won't get paid for your stupidity.

You have to stop being in such a hurry to do nothing. When you rush, you tend to ignore small details which will lead to problems sooner or later. Besides, when you take your time, you are able to see and do things better.

BANs first glances at the glass, sees it as half empty, and immediately starts bitching about how much they have left. Not one thought of thanks of "at least I have something to drink." People can be ungrateful ass bitches! People are dying of thirst, and a nigga sitting here complaining about a half cup of juice. Bitches with attitude like that really do not deserve shit because they are always wanting shit done their way when they say it but they can't even control their own attitude. Just know, they are simpleminded motherfuckers that love to manipulate people.

You should not want to go through life without taking any risks. Don't be that nigga talking about "I wish I could win this or hit the lotto," but do not play shit.

It is hard being uncomfortable, but if you look at it this way, the more uncomfortable you are the more comfortable you will be in being uncomfortable. You are uncomfortable because you are not sure of the outcome, but you should not worry if you truly believe in self. If someone has to tell you to do it, then it is not in you. It takes a team to win, but someone else shouldn't constantly have to tell you how to live your life.

Everything in life happens to you to build the you that you need to be. Don't go through life looking at shit as bad all the time. Sometimes, things happen to you to let you know what it is you like and things you don't like. And sometimes, bad shit tends to happen to make you stronger for tasks you have ahead. Remember, experiences and knowledge are tools to help you along the journey. You have to pull the right tool out at the right time for the right situation to be able move through life the right way and get things done.

Living a life without direction is like being granted a plane and you are the pilot, my friend. Imagine you are flying, enjoying life, flying across the water with a plane full of fuel. Eventually that fuel hand will start to slowly make its way down after flying freely through the skies. Soon you will have to land or you will run into some serious trouble. If you have some guidance, direction—a map or GPS—you have the ability to land, fill up, get straight back in the sky, and go free again. Without a clear point of direction, you are just flying aimlessly with no idea where you are going or what will happen once you get there. You have to know where you are headed and not just be cloud watching. You have to have some type of idea of what the fuck is going on. Not being aware of your surroundings, not caring where you are or where you are going, is a pointless pursuit and a reckless endeavor. It has the potential to harm either you or someone else. When you think about it, that is a dangerous person to be or be around.

Looking at Shit in Different Ways

Suppose you stop by a store to get yourself some chips, but before you go in the store you ask Bae if she wants something and she says no. So, you proceed to do what you do and come out with chips. Once opening the chips, before you even put your hand in the bag, Bae's hand is in the bag. I know you're saying...*well, it's only a bag of chips*...which is correct, but Bae could've spoken up as well. Now if you would've slapped that hand down and asked her what she was doing, it would've been WWIII, but never turn to violence over petty shit. If you pull up for happy hour, why not get two drinks when you know somebody's deep-throat ass is going to get greedy? You can look at this as being minor, but little things turn to big things. You may not like sharing everything when you can get two the first time. It will be times where you do share things, but it will also be times where you want the whole sucker. It is called entitlement and you have watch that behavior, because it can carry on to how a person acts out in the world. You have to make Bae say what they mean and mean what they say.

One thing you need to understand is that the chain is only as good its links. No one is perfect by any means. Neither should you try to make them out to be, but it's cool to call someone on their flaws if you are trying to build them up or trying to build a team. As a team, if one member is weak, then it weakens the whole group. A team is only as strong as its weakest member, so if you want a strong team, then you have to make sure that you put strong members on it.

Only tear down if you plan to rebuild. If you are not rebuilding, then the energy you're using is useless and can be put toward something else constructive. We always find ourselves staring at the problem when that is really the problem, because now you're just in the way, gossiping about the negative because you just want to stay negative. Instead, figure out a way to make a change for the better. Do things to enhance, not destroy. And if you only stare at a problem without doing anything to fix it, then the problem just becomes worse and you might as well say you helped it.

Always focus on the solution and work on that. BANs are the weak links but are not always easily seen. Being in a relationship with one can blind you to the faults that you would normally pay attention to and not take. You need to know the signs and be aware because they are toxic and need to be addressed immediately. Ignoring the dead-end sign half a mile back won't do you any good ahead. That is why you should always pay attention to details because it will paint the whole picture for you if you let it. Let's say you and Bae are riding and you are driving. You stop at an intersection where pedestrians are crossing and some are taking their time. All of a sudden, Bae starts laying on the horn, knowing damn well she can't fight. The pedestrians look at you like *what the fuck is your problem*. At this very moment, your Bae just put you in a fucked-up situation that can go left at any time because she is reckless and feels entitled because you can handle it when it's all said and done. You may get out of this situation easily, no problem. Now, you can continue to let Bae keep blowing the horn from the passenger seat and keep taking the blame or train Bae to be a passenger only and let you be the driver. And if Bae's ass can't cash the check that her mouth keeps writing, then it's best to know when to shut the fuck up because not all people will let you keep selling wolf tickets.

Weak links have the tendency to use passive-aggressive tactics. Passive-aggression means indirect resistance to the demand of others and the avoidance of direct confrontation, as in pouting or hiding someone's important shit and some bitches even use fake-crying. Overlook these tactics and know they just do this so you will leave it along for peace sake, which is something you don't want to encourage because it will bite you later. It is called kicking the can down the road.

It can be good to be stubborn if you are standing for the right thing, but know that you can be easily distracted when standing for the right call. You get right and make people feel left behind, and they make you question yourself if you are doing right because they are looking at you differently. It's like they think you are in the wrong for trying to better yourself and leaving them out.

Everyone has the same 24 hours. How do you use yours? Always pull from that gut feeling and fuck the rest. You have to know you can't fill a bucket with a hole in it. Never let anyone stop you from improving your life.

Stubborn can be the ugly side of perseverance. A BAN will be contrary just because he can. He feeds off playing games with your emotions. It's the highlight of his day because he has nothing else to look forward to. Talking to a stubborn BAN can be dangerous if you don't watch it. A stubborn BAN will go along with the opposite of what you are saying just because they get some satisfaction out of getting to you. If BANs can see they're is getting to you, that is nothing but gas to their emotions to keep being goofy. You must not let foolishness get you worked up and make you respond in any kind to his foolery. The best way to handle a situation like this is always to remain calm. Never let a BAN know that they can affect your emotions. The minute a BAN knows he can drag you down to his level and play his game, he knows he's got you right where he wants you—under his control. One thing you cannot do is beat a BAN at his own game, because there is no cap to a BAN's bullshit. If you remain relaxed and let the BAN know that that bullshit doesn't faze you, eventually he will back off and move on.

BANs are typically scared of confrontation nor do they want to be left open with the chance of being rejected. BANs are really not sure of themselves: they lack confidence. They will do things to test just how far you will let them go, how much you will let them get away with. There's a scene in the first *Jurassic Park* movie where the characters are discussing the Tyrannosaurus Rex. They are told that she will constantly touch different parts of the electric fence to check for any weaknesses. Like this T-Rex, a BAN will constantly test you, looking for your weak points to exploit, using them against you to get whatever he wants from you.

At all moments, a BAN is looking to see what level of bitch he has you at, and based off your reactions, it will tell him exactly where you stand. BANs act off energy or emotion whether good or bad. It doesn't matter. They just need it. It is like blood to a vampire. A BAN just has to get a reaction out your ass.

Now, there's nothing wrong with being nice and serving others, but some BANs get shit fucked up. You have to be careful showing hospitality to a nigga who doesn't appreciate or deserve it. Stop giving BANs energy when it's causing you pain. Remember, BANs run off energy whether it is good or bad. Kill the energy: kill the BAN.

Learn how to think before reacting. Never use emotion as judgment because it normally gets you in a fucked-up position. You are all up in your feelings and not at your true state of being. Stop freely giving emotions to these bitches, feeding them life. Your time and emotions should be priceless and not just given away so easily. If you don't use your time wisely, someone else will use it for you, and it might not be in the way you want it to be.

Check this out: you're chilling, minding your damn business. All of a sudden, you hear someone ask *do you work tomorrow*, *are you going somewhere tomorrow*, or *are you doing anything tomorrow*. Those questions are thrown at you as stepping-stone questions. These are open questions that lead up to the real problem, which is controlling your every move. There are many roads you can go down when being hit with these types of bullshit police question. You can answer the questions and truly say what your plans are or you can ask why or what is on his mind. Understand that these questions were thrown at you to set you up for the killer question, which is them trying to know your every move. So, by answering these types of police questions, you are setting yourself up for some bullshit you might not want to deal with.

For some reason, a BAN believes that, just because you are off work, it means you are off to do whatever the fuck he wants you to do. You fuck around and tell him you're off or chilling, and before you know it, a BAN has a whole to-do list for your ass. In the back of your mind, you're thinking you said you're off or chilling, not looking for work to do. To stop this scene from happening, just make him be direct and stop stalling and ask what he really wants to know. You have to stop enabling a BAN in controlling you and all of the situations you find yourself in with him.

Everything should not go their way. Relationships should be partnerships that benefit both parties involved. At the end of the day, you need to start saying what you're feeling. But remember, every action has a reaction, so be willing and ready to receive the reaction behind that shit. However, when you start to exercise that action, you'll start to feel better because holding your feelings in is like poison to the body. You have spit that shit out and man or woman the fuck up and take some responsibility and speak up for yourself.

You have to practice not to give a fuck when BANs play mind games. If they are playing games with you, why give a fuck about saying how you feel? Don't let a person pick your mind apart so easily. Start asking why, or use other types of responses to help keep people from just giving you shit to do or make it so easy to put stuff on you. Make a BAN have a reason for asking questions or doing something.

A person should not flow through life making moves with no reason behind it. Every move should be made with the mindset that there is a consequence behind your actions, and ask yourself if you are willing to make that boss decision.

If it is just as simple as a question like *what are you doing today*, your response should be a simple why. You should not be mad at people for asking question, but if it is these BANs then, after they ask a question and you answer it with a nothing, and then you ask why, their response will usually be, "Nothing, just asking." They are asking for reason though: they are plotting. Stop that shit at the gate with a why: always ask why they are asking. Make them spill the beans. See what is on their mind first before you show your cards and stop a bitch from playing with your mind while setting you up for a game you may not want to play. A person could be wanting to do something nice and mean good, but never let a bitch start asking set-up questions or jab questions to see how you react. Make them ask what they really want to ask and stop wasting your time.

At times, it seems like a BAN is always stepping on your toes, telling you what you're doing, what you need to be doing, and what you're not doing. A BAN always sees fault, while also leaving a trail of bullshit that you could be petty about but choose to go the nice route. Going the nice route by letting shit slide for peace sake is a violation to self. You should never let bullshit slide, whether big or small because small turns into big. It is a must that you take shit head on with a BAN. It is a must that you address all the bullshit as it comes your way. It may seem small-minded or petty, but in order to establish some ground, address the shit as it is happening. Don't wait to bring the shit up the next week or some other later date.

Don't bring up old shit like a BAN. Let the past stay in the past and move on. Check this out: if you constantly address the bullshit BANs bring as it is happening, then they can see the shit they are doing more easily. BANs have the tendency to pick at your flaws so much they forget, or want you to ignore, the bullshit they do. BANs stay busy grilling you so that you don't have time or energy to grill them. If you let shit slide and only bring it up in a discussion later, you will feel defeated because a BAN will never remember or admit to old shit.

The spotlight in a BAN's head will only be on whatever you are being called out on. BANs always let shit go in one ear and out the other; sometimes, they make you will feel like you are talking to a brick wall. That is why you address the shit as it happening to let the BAN see he has flaws, too. And you do it while they are in action where they cannot deny it. Think of it as only making the chain stronger by exposing each other's weaknesses.

While picking at each other, if you don't have a solution, then you really should shut the fuck up. Why tear someone down if you are not going to build them back up and make them stronger? BANs walk around interested in only finding problems, not finding solutions. If you address something, have a reason for addressing it. If you don't start addressing shit and saying what is deep down in your gut to set the tone, standards, or boundaries early on in the relationship, it can be hard correcting it later on. If someone has been getting an hour for lunch, it is hard to take that person down to thirty minutes.

Don't be that person who watches somebody do something wrong when you could have prevented it from happening but your scary ass is too much of a bitch to say what is on your mind. A BAN normally just watches and lets shit play out to see the disaster just for some type of inside amusement.

Being Handicapped

Every past has a future and every future has a past. With that being said, you can wipe your ass with those excuses on why the fuck you're not living life to your fullest potential. Maybe you need to start looking at what you do regularly, how you spend your time, and with whom you usually surround yourself. Just stop reading for a second and think to yourself what is it besides gossiping, watching tv, and playing on social media that you do to build yourself on the regular. Your normal answer is probably nothing, because you're waiting on these piles of money that supposed to fall at any time from the sky. That is an unrealistic dream. You need to get up and work. Hard work always pays off and always outlasts the weak. Stop waiting on someone to do something for you and do it for yourself.

In life, you have people who will either will run to success or run from it. Think of an estimate of how much money you have in the bank and decide whether or not you deserve to be taking a break, sleeping all day. The people who are getting money stay busy all day. It seems to them it is not enough time in a day, yet your bitch ass is complaining about not having enough sleep time. Everyone has 24 hours in a day. What are you doing with yours besides looking at it? There is no time for not being productive, just not doing shit in life. Real men stand up, don't make excuses, and make shit happen. Real men don't blame another nigga for their lacking. Real men take on responsibility because that is what the fuck they do. That is why they get the big piece of the fucking chicken. Boys need to get some fire put up under their asses to be something besides just another leech on someone else's success.

There is absolutely no excuse not to be working. You can flip burgers or hold a sign and dance. Real men know it's *fuck your pride, get a check*. When I say fuck your pride, I mean we, as people, can have so much pride that we'd rather take no money instead of what we can get right now to eat. This is why it is important to add value to yourself. If you add value to yourself, people will pay your worth. Value is nothing that you just say or just place on you. Value is something that people view as important, helpful, beneficial, and respectful. We all know respect is something that you earn by putting in the work to receive it. When people say they've been looking two months for a job, it cannot be allowed to be used as an excuse. So, two months you've been bringing in no money, just taking up space in the world, getting in everyone else's way who is trying to get some. If you really want to have a job, then you can hustle. You can wash cars: 5 cars a day for $20 a car = $100, times 5 days = $500 weekly. That is $2,000 a month while still job searching. No matter what you choose, as long as it is legal, you can always find a hustle to generate some income.

No one should support anyone else's habits. Asking for loose cigarettes, shorts, and shit is some bum type shit. How is it you smoke but don't have smoke and can't afford no smoke? The same thing applies to the drinkers. Get off your asses and grind for what you want. That way, when you get it, you will appreciate it that much more. After a long day or week of hard work, you deserve a reward of drink, smoke, sex—whatever you desire—but for a BAN to sit around, don't do shit but complain about the weather is some sucker ass shit. For the bitches out there who allow this shit to go on, you deserve what you get. Don't let a sorry BAN sit at home while you work and make shit happen. I didn't say women because women know better. Bitches don't know better, so those are the ones that need someone to slap some sense in their head. You can't do better if you don't know better.

If you don't work, you don't play. Simple as that. Men handle business then relax and play when they can. Boys should be checked to see if they are doing homework before playing outside. And by homework, I mean working for things to bring to the table that the household needs or can benefit from. Niggas get comfortable so quickly these days, or either these bitches are letting their standards down. When I say comfortable, that means niggas do the minimum to get by just so they won't look like a scrub.

Too few people want to take that extra step to invest in themselves instead of everyone else. Only thing you are elevating is debt. Get some money: stop borrowing shit when you're not even going to pay it back. When you get some money, save some of that shit. First, pay bills because that is what grown people do. Adults carry their own weight. Adults put needs before wants. You buy purses and shoes for 4 or 5 hundred dollars and then only have $23 in your account, or eating the 4 for $4 and your gas light stay on, plus you need your oil changed and a front-end alignment asap, but your spending your money like you think it's endless.

Today, we have Shawty with red bottom shoes on but walking the red off them. We have buddy Gucci/Louis mix, high designer, but he lives at home with his mom and doesn't have a driver's license. Our priorities are all fucked up and need to be examined. Staying at home with your parents or anywhere and paying no bills—you don't have the right to be fucked up. A phone, a car, and over $2,500 in an account are just the basics if you have no responsibilities. Don't just fuck off all your money and never plan to leave the nest. You can't be sheltered or relying on people to do things for you. When your ass is left in the spotlight with no help, some people can't take it and hang it up. Don't be that person. Waiting on somebody to take you somewhere can be frustrating, but you can go and leave as you please in your own shit. Stop waiting on a meal and cook a meal. Adults take care of themselves and don't rely on Mom and Dad or any type of sponsorship to fund their lifestyle.

There is no excuse not to be trying to do something to better yourself. Nothing is worse than a nigga who always need a ride, always short on his end. BANs are always looking for somebody else to fill in the gaps that they don't want to fill.

Stop waiting to die without leaving 30 miles outside your address. Experience some shit in life besides living it through that damn phone.

Stop buying all these nice cars if you are parking it at Mom's house or fighting for parking spots at these cheap ass apartments. Nice shit should be kept in a garage, and not just any garage but your garage. It is so much better to have an A to B car and have your own shit. Having your own shit comes with responsibilities like bills and the maintenance of shit.

If your money doesn't agree with it, why are you forcing it? All the time, you know your money is yelling, "My nigga, we're not ready yet. Let a nigga grow a little bit first." But no, your ass balls out anyway, then be needing money for lunch tomorrow and to survive the rest of the week. Your priority should be paying bills first, filling up your gas tank, buying food, and saving at least a dollar or two in the oh-shit box. Shit always tends to happen when we least expect it, and nothing is better than having something saved for when that oh-shit moment happens and we need help. Oh-shit moments are for emergency reasons, not because-I-want-to-eat at Friday's. It is for you to go to first before you go begging with nothing when you need help. You still may not get any help, but at least you have a start.

The point is not to live above your money. Money is like fruit. You have to plant it and tend to it to put it in motion to get it coming in. You have to plant something to survive. You have to let shit grow until it is ready. If you pull it early, it is mostly going to be bitter, unpleasant, and sour, not to anyone's liking. The same occurs with money spent and not saved up until it's ready. So, how about we start planting these seeds of money and knowledge, let them grow, and then eat when it's ready? Doing this can help build a backbone for yourself and can free you from being someone else's dead weight.

Wanting a Rose but not Respecting the Thorns

Almost everyone has that dream of finding that sexy ass person to marry, to look at and get butterflies and shit when that person comes around. They believe this will fulfill them in life, but it is all about balance. Women want a man with a lot of money and a lot of time. Men want a freaky girl with no miles. Not saying they are not out there: I'm just saying they are slim. That is why you must find a good balance that fits you best. A guy can work all day to get the money, but never have time to spend it with you. We want a career-minded woman but can't handle the challenge that comes with it. All things I said were wants when we need to be on what we need. We need to slow down and get our shit together.

No two people on this earth are completely alike. Everyone is unique in his or her own way by nature. It makes you special and that much more valuable. Someone can be good at spending money and someone can be good at saving money. Everyone needs that balance.

In today's society, we want shit now, and damn, I mean now. Hell, who don't want it now? We're raising the next generation to be a microwave society where everything is done quickly and we get it super-fast, from food to relationships to the items we buy. But the fastest is not always the best, and all the greats know that whatever is built to last takes some patience and time. If it doesn't work right, the smallest piece, such as a spark plug on a car, can shut something down and will not let it move. So, when making decisions, always pay attention to details, because we tend to look over those details until we have made a decision and pretty much stuck in it. Then, you're sitting there with the I-was-in-my-feelings face.

That is why it is important to slow down and take your time because no one knows the background, the process, the day-after-day input it took for your rose to grow, and ladies, you are roses. All we know is that a rose is beautiful, and it gives us a sense of joy, fulfilment, balance, and love. But do you really care about the rose or what it represents? Or do you just care about what others think about your rose or the ability to get a rose. Life is supposed to be filled with love, balance, and joy...that new car smell and feeling. It's a wonderful feeling, but it doesn't come simple. In the life of roses, some people think that just because they know where the rose garden is, they can go rip them a rose by hand, running away and screaming, jumping up in joy. "I got a rose! I got a rose!" Everyone rushes to show their rose off, so they will know that you, too, can get a rose. That shit looks cool with pics on social media, but offline, they're struggling to keep the rose. Not thinking of the process that your impatient ass took to get a rose, you didn't notice that you may have rushed in too quickly to pick it or that your hands are bleeding from the thorns. The petals are half gone due to the roughness, swinging, and the plucking you did before you can get it home and take care of it. Most of you don't even have the time, patience, or the drive to deserve a rose. It takes special care and a gentle hand to provide for a rose. Anything less, and the rose will eventually die.

Technology can make you believe you are something that you are really not. You think you're keeping up with the Joneses but the Joneses filing bankruptcy like a motherfucker. In most cases, the Joneses are faking their lifestyle. A lot of time, the people who wear these expensive things are sponsored by those people and fool us to pay top dollar for cheap shit, so let's not get caught up in that material competition with each other. Only be in competition with yourself.

You should always have respect and dignity in what you do. What you do is a reflection of you. Always take time and plan your work and work your plan. Always make your next move the best move. The decisions that we make stick with us for the rest of our lives and sometimes after that.

In today's society violence is the new norm. You should never put your hands on anyone. Who is making these niggas hit women, catching bitch fits and all in their feelings, getting emotional about everything? People who mentally and physically abuse women normally don't want to cry and don't know how to express themselves or are scared to, so a BAN hits and abuses people because he feels backed into a corner where his strength is all he has to show he is a man. He's normally an old, insecure ass nigga with hidden secrets he is running from. Only a bitch ass nigga tests his strength on a female. He believes that the consequences are low for his bitch moves. Bitch ass niggas are scared of a challenge, so they pick on weak and defenseless women. All the men that like combat are in that UFC boxing-type shit with other crazy motherfuckers going through shit and can defend themselves and get paid to do that shit. There are times when a bitch's elevator really doesn't go all the way to the top and your woman is strengthening your life. A nigga can get cornered on some it-is-me-or-you type shit where you may have to disarm the crazy hoe. Should you be in the hospital for being nice to someone with a weapon or should you disarm them and fuck what happens during the process if something happens to them? Apparently, the BAN didn't care about you or his life in the first place.

Understand that it is not the guy's fault all the time. Some of these bitches be so aggressive and confrontational these days. Some of them act like they are niggas, and when she gets treated like one, then the bitch wants to play the I'm-a-woman card. There are no rules in street fighting. A nigga needs to do whatever it takes to defend himself. Don't make it have to be one of those so-you-gone-shoot-me-in-my-pinky-toe moments from Harlem Nights.

Women are so delicate and beautiful. There is no way a woman can withstand the blows of a real man nor would she want to. Women are too fragile to be mishandled in the first place. Women are like roses, built to defend not attack. So, women, don't engage in jumping in his face, hitting him, throwing things at him, or verbally hitting below the belt. Your calling him out of his name or telling all those secrets he told you when he was drunk or during pillow talk is inexcusable. Stop engaging in the theatrics, and learn how to defend not attack. Defend only when attacked because, when you are stuck in defensive mode, you can never get chosen. Being a rose means to be beautiful and full of joy and balance, not all that ratchet-ass shit, just being reckless, making noise to get attention, damn near about to kill yourself to get a like. Don't act like a man if you don't want to be treated like a man. I know some of you tough-back bitches think you can, but you should not want to.

   If a nigga hits you once, I advise to you leave. The chances are too high that he will do it again. Ask yourself why should you take that risk when this nigga just bruised up your beautiful face, got you in the bathroom transforming your face to hide the bruises from people at your job because you can't call in. So why let a couple of I'm-sorry's, some flowers, and all kinds of I-fucked-up gifts line you up for round 2? It is okay to forgive and love if you choose, but choose to give that love to someone else who deserves it, especially yourself. Have respect for yourself. The best lesson for a person after he has whooped your ass and bruised you up physically or emotionally is to leave and stay gone. He will tell you he's sorry and that you are the best thing that's ever happened to him and the only one who understands him. It's all an act to win you back. Let that BAN go. Never fuck with him again. Make him regret that he fucked up. If he really regrets it, then the next relationship he gets in, he will have learned to control that bitch inside him.

The best lesson is a bought lesson. If a nigga see he can get away with something like that and there are no consequences, he will definitely do it again. The same goes for females. Even though there are some guys who need to be slapped upside their damn heads and grow some nuts, everyone should keep their hands to themselves unless in an intimate way. It should never be to a point of physical abuse because a BAN can't control himself. No way I'm going to sleep with a bitch I just whooped and expect to wake up. Some BANs tend to hit women as a reflection to what bitches be saying because they feel as if they are cornered, making them feel defenseless as a man, so they show they are men by using their physical power. But there is never a good reason for a grown man to hit a woman.

In today's society, women are running shit and not looking back. Women are now holding it down without a nigga. Only a BAN needs someone to hold him down. See, when a beautiful, strong, and educated sista comes off as aggressive or independent, nothing is wrong with that. You are a rose. You can't help what you are. BANs who complain or say negative things are the niggas who don't deserve a rose. A rose has to be given light, water, and love. A BAN can't provide that. When you are an expensive piece of equipment, only those who can't afford you or don't know how to handle you are intimidated and scared.

I want to point out that there's a certain group of bitches that believe in their pastor more than they do in their man. You encourage your pastor more than your man. It takes your pastor to validate what your man is saying. Respect your man. Respect is the gas to his mind. You have to praise short-bus-shawty even if short-bus-shawty just doing the bare minimum. Just keep cheering. Always talk high of your man. That shit makes him feel damn good, like sex. It is pretty much foreplay for a guy. To be talked highly of. To be praised, and to be looked up to. That sense of need. All men desire it. Motivate each other and really listen to what each other says.

Just respect the rose and the thorns. Handle the rose with care and nurture it. Before you choose, take your time and choose carefully. Know if you have what it takes to keep a rose alive.

Causes and Effect: Surface Happiness

Being happy is not always the easiest thing because every day is a challenge, especially when you have someone else attached to you emotionally. It is hard enough to keep yourself level with the fast pace of society because there is something new every day. Technology will really put pressure on you in a good way or bad way because everything is so open and quick-moving. There is really no privacy at all any more: everything is for the public to see. Any and everything is being exposed or tricked with social media. Simpleminded people walk around with the aim to be messy, waiting on some TMZ or World Star type shit to look at and get some quick cool points off a nigga. Keep in mind, it is always a nigga out there coming for you that just won't let you make it. Don't take it wrong. Some people look at your life and wish they could spend 24 hours in your shoes or just hate it is you. You're crazy if you think people- don't pay attention to your pockets and how you move.

Being in a relationship can be challenging too, if you let it. You can make that shit hard or you can make that shit easy. Being in a relationship is a full-time job. So, if you think you can put in part-time work and get full-time pay, you've got life fucked up. And if you think this way, you are the reason this book was written. If you think of this from a business standpoint, what will you do or how will you feel?

If a BAN starts to pull no-call no-shows, they will real soon be fired. They clock in when they're ready; and when they do clock in, they complain but want a full week work's worth check on Friday. The crazy part is when BANs see a trainee starting their first day, they get all worked up because now their services could possibly no longer be needed. You know how temp services do. So, when BANs get fired, they want you to feel sorry for them, but you must not. BANs will give you a million excuses why they can't come to work and a million reasons why not to fire them.

A relationship is work. I mean actually acknowledging each other and being productive in a relationship, so make sure you are in a real relationship. Just because we're fucking, it doesn't make us a couple. Just fucking makes you a temp worker. Don't confuse temps as full-time employees with benefits. Be very clear what you have. Never assume because the pay is totally different.

Excuses are simple. "Hey, I know I did wrong, but here is the reason I did wrong even though I know what I was doing is wrong but listen to this excuse and give a nigga a pass. Nobody's perfect." By saying that, they know they did wrong. With that being said, it is best that one saves the excuses and take responsibility, like you should. So, if you are running a business, how would you run it? Would it be a nice, healthy environment or an unstable, hostile one?

It is always important to think about and weigh the consequences of any decision because the consequences can be more damaging than the decision that was made. That is why this faithful shit is not common these days, but there are good people looking for a good healthy relationship and not all about bullshit drama in a relationship. Let's be 100: if you don't have a ring or papers on that dick or pussy, my nigga, then it is fair game, so hope for the best. If another person comes through and catches you lacking in different departments, he will take what you thought you had. It is best that you take that shit like a G and understand you have no papers on this bitch, no titles. So why stress, young grasshopper? Let someone else have that problem.

If someone takes your spouse, then she wasn't really for you anyway. Why try to find a reason for someone to fuck you over? If John or Suzy is a BAN why continue to be with a BAN? You know a BAN is all for self. A BAN doesn't have time to be thinking about the rules and principles of a relationship. That is why it is important to know who you've got. And don't ignore the signs, especially if the signs smack you in the face, which they normally do: we just ignore the shit. Once people show you who they are, believe that shit. If you want to know what a person is really like, give them money or power. Give a BAN either one of those, and the true character will reveal itself, and when it does, believe it.

BANs tend to hold shit in until money or power come into play, because when you are weak or broke, you are not secure like you are supposed to be. So, when power and money come, you just become the person you always wanted to be but never had the courage to when you thought you were weak or broke. Always know your value, and stick to the principles and law inside of you.

In the go-together game, you need to understand, my nigga, y'all just fucking and enjoying life trying to figure out what you like and what you don't like. It is encouraging to experience different types of people. You should really be open to dating many people. Not fucking many people but dating, as in getting to know them. You should really stay focused on yourself until you can manage yourself. No need to get in something if you are not complete. If you do that, then you become a burden to someone else. You become needy if you're not complete.

If you're not complete, you can find yourself in a fucked-up situation because temptation can catch up. Temptation always comes when we are at our weakest or when we are confused. When you don't know you, you can fall for anything somebody tells you.

In a relationship, the number one thing is trust. If you don't trust me, then why be with me? Why be with someone you don't trust? How can you receive love when you are so closed? Never come to play if you are not fully willing to play. If you're having trouble with past shit, then maybe it is you. Maybe you need to go sit down and reflect on what you've been doing. Maybe you need some alone time. Learn how to be by yourself before entertaining anyone. You don't want to stress yourself wondering if he is fucking on the job or if she is still letting the ex-boyfriend knock the bottom out that ass, sending her back to you with nut leaking out her pussy, and now she wants to act as if her head hurting and not feeling well to keep from fucking you because her other friend went balls deep this time and she's sore. Maybe tomorrow you'll get some after she recovers and puts some snap back on that pussy for you. People live through crazy shit like that and then wonder why their health and mental stability is off.

Being in a relationship should not be stressful at all. We seem to make shit harder than it has to be. It's all about not ignoring the signs and paying attention to detail. This is very important to remember and understand: if you go to the park or anyplace where your ass can dig up some dirt and actually start digging that shit up, go through it. I guarantee you're going to find some shit. I don't know what you will find, but you're going find something. Same thing in your life. If you take your nosy ass and go digging through someone's phone and social media accounts, I guarantee you're going to find something to have issue with. It may not be anything serious, but you will build a case around it anyway. It is just you wanting to start something because you know your ass is not shit.

Pay attention to this and understand. Being at the beach can be lovely. You can walk and feel the sand go through your feet while you are just enjoying the moment. Always live in the moment. If you ever notice, the ocean always washes thing up on the shore—from shells and debris to any and everything a motherfucker can possibly be doing out there. Most of the time, it will eventually wash up and present itself to you without you putting in any effort. Now if you go scuba diving and snorkeling—all that nosy shit—and go looking for shit and fuck around get eaten by shark, being a little nosy bitch, you have to understand, you are out of line. The water is not for you to go diving for shit unless you are fully equipped. Stay where you have control and where you are enjoying yourself. Whatever a nigga or bitch is out there doing will eventually wash up.

You have to trust and believe in what you have. You always know what you have. We like to ignore the shit, but remember, however you came in the relationship plays a major role in how you maintain one. It's always good to reflect on how y'all came about. Maybe emotions were involved and you could see shit clearer than you can now. If we know who we have, then we don't have to inspect them; instead, we appreciate them.

If you are happy, why go looking for sadness? Especially if you're not going any damn where. Why kill a good vibe by looking for shit you don't want to find, then when you find something out, you're ready to go jump off a bridge, you big dummy? A BAN just doesn't want to be happy. If you are happy why go looking for mess unless the shit is in your face? If that happens, then you check that shit on site not later. It has always been said if you didn't actually touch them, it wasn't them. It's look-alike out here, so fuck your pic cause they photoshopping every day.

Even if a nigga is innocent, a BAN can sneak in quick and innocent. A BAN slides in the DM of your loved one and ask how your best friend or cousin is doing as a distraction to get them to respond easily. They do, and then your nosy ass come digging, and now he or she is cheating over some petty convo. You have to understand you can't control what these hating ass people are going to do. They believe in keeping you from being happy if you let them. People are going to do whatever they want to do, and it is nothing you can do about it. You will kill yourself stalking a person, plus that shit is creepy, insecure, and going to get your ass in a revolving door of sadness, if not dead.

Always know your value. People always take care of the people or things we put value on. If you feel as if you are not valued, then move the fuck on with life. It's your choice, young whippersnapper. Don't get caught up on thoughts like *we have put so much time in already, we make this power couple,* or whatever. When you're not valued, leave.

Check this out. Do you really want somebody that don't nobody else want? You should give yourself an evaluation if don't nobody else want your mate. The chances are you have a wild grizzly, and nobody has the time deal with him but you, which can be a good thing because there is someone for everybody. You just have to run into them. But if your boo is any kind of good-looking, it should be all types of motherfuckers getting at them on the daily to keep you on your shit. You just don't get a Ferrari-type ride and don't get any attention. All types of BANs will be coming up taking pics and touching it, trying to steal it. BANs will aggressively be asking questions, just flocking from everywhere. Well it's the same with your boo. The more valuable your boo is the more attention comes that way and the more aware you have to be on what is going on and not have your eyes closed. Always stay tuned to your number one.

Show Horse vs Work Horse

Life is all about choices. Everyone has some and have to make them whether or not they want to. When we make these choices, you must understand what it is you're choosing.

Everything in life worth having requires tending to. Anything worth having requires being groomed and having regular maintenance. Even a tree requires maintenance. For some people, the grass always seems to look better at the other house. There, the grass looks all green and soft. But it's supposed to look like that! Nobody has signs posted of their lowdown dealings. The whole time you're being jealous of someone else's lawn and the grass could be fake. Even if it is real, you don't know what people are doing for the upkeep of their lawn either. They're probably struggling with issues you have no idea about to get a lawn that looks that good. They may have had to work all kinds of hours to produce the lawn that you now see. You see the product but have no idea of the price that had to be paid.

Don't get pressured or distracted by people who flash presents and shit on social media and now you think you have to top the bar. Most people who do that shit be receiving those I'm-sorry-I-know-I'm-not-shit-but-please-take-me-back gifts. You do it when you have fucked up: we all do. But to the nigga that shit is straight disrespectful. It makes you want to high-five their face in your mind. Nigga start getting roses, expensive gifts, joining the choir even though they haven't been to church in years—shit they wouldn't normally do. We see it time after time. They take the gifts along with the BAN and flash them to the audience to prove that Bae really is not a little ain't-shit bitch so she won't look bad from getting disrespected. This is straight foolishness and won't last in the long run.

Always stay focused on what you have and take care of it. A show horse is nice and pretty. Everyone likes to ride it, rub it, and take pictures of it. There's nothing wrong with a show horse if that is what you like, but you should want your taste buds to match your bank account. You know us niggas, we want shit, but can't afford it most of the time, and knowing damn well it is not a good idea, we tell ourselves fuck it and get it anyways. Later, we're like *what the fuck was I thinking signing my life away.*

That it is why you have to be careful stepping on that emotional rollercoaster. When our emotions take over, we do some silly shit that we will regret later, stuff that we normally wouldn't even think about doing. A show horse requires a lot of upkeep, a lot money, and a lot of work if you want it to stay a show horse, because that is what it is, not a work horse. We sometimes try to get shit, then tweak it to us to say we have it, too. You know like you go get a 300 and try to convince ourselves it's a Rolls Royce. We be doing the most.

Having a show horse is money consuming with no real benefits to your life. You're really just paying a person for the upkeep of a certain lifestyle to make you look good. Show horses are really for ballers who can afford to pay other people to take care of the horses for them, but you know us niggas have to do it ourselves trying to save money when we should have never fucked with it in the first place. To keep up with the Joneses is our downfall. You have to spend a lot of time grooming the horses and taking care of them. You pretty much are treating them as if they are babies. A show horse doesn't produce shit but attention and some likes. Now if we get paid to show, then that's another story, but we have to be making a profit, not be losing.

Try to look at everything like a business. If we are not making money, how can we continue to be able to show? If it's constantly withdraw, withdraw, withdraw, withdraw and no deposit, eventually you're going to bankrupt or overdraft. A show horse is really dead weight if you don't have the funds to enjoy it, because without the funds, it becomes time and money consuming with really nothing to get out of it but a headache. People that have the money can pay someone else to groom and take care of the horse, and they just show it. So, if a show horse is what you want, then understand the responsibilities of owning it and take the responsibility and shut the fuck up about the choice you made.

Now a workhorse is totally different but still requires grooming and being taken care of. It is easier to care for and is there for you instead of waiting on you. A workhorse helps move that dead weight that one person can't just do alone or should not have to do alone. With help we get at least twice as far if not farther because you have someone to motivate you in a sense, so why not have help. A workhorse is built to work. A workhorse helps in ways that, if you were doing something alone, with its help, you get things done sooner and make it easier on your body and mind. If you have to choose a horse, why not a workhorse that can help bring some improvement to your life, not just bring attention and also cost you? That workhorse is meant to be in the sun, sweating and using muscle, unlike a show horse that will fall out doing work because it needs to be pampered.

Having help always gets the job done faster. Help is always easier on the muscles. Help is good for mental health as well as physical health. The main thing you need in life to succeed is help. The choice is yours. Just remember, everything that looks good is not good for you or the best fit for you. Think about your money status or the lifestyle you are trying to get to before you decide which horse you really need. Remember, they are not mandatory. They are just assets and are supposed to add to life more than subtract from, or eventually they will just become a liability.

There's no time for people who are looking for a handout. People go through shit and some people stay in that shit. Some niggas do try to make ends meet, but life has some way of upper cutting them with the bullshit at the wrong time. A real hustler type will keep trying shit like flipping burgers and a part-time job here and there, always grinding. A nigga doing something to make something doesn't deserve to be compared to a BAN selling you pipe dreams while living finger-licking good off most of these bitches. Watch these niggas that think they look better than you in a relationship, unless these niggas get paid to look good, and still watch them.

Adults add to your life not suck it out you. Bitches have to stop sponsoring these niggas since Nike or Reebok not sending offers. Ladies, these BANs are not your responsibility to be putting together and taking care of them. That BAN has a mom already. If a person won't take care of himself, who do you think he is going to rely on when he gets with you? We live in a different time from when one person could hold it down. Shit, now it takes two people to exist. In order to have something, you have to be with somebody who also wants something. You can do bad by yourself, so if you're struggling alone, keep being alone. Your mate should motivate you to stay on your shit because they are on their shit. The game plan should be to win. Get someone who helps and wants to go to the same levels as you. Don't get caught trying to drag dead weight to levels only you're trying to get to because now it will take double the work getting there.

When your partner is bitching, a.k.a getting on your ass, they just see the lacking in the weak and want the chain to stay strong. But a BAN will let emotions cloud his judgment and get in his feelings. A BAN can't take constructive criticism. When backing out, if you tell your partner to let the car stop then put it in drive and go, he doesn't listen. Instead, he's revving in neutral before you can put it in drive and then he wonders why their transmission is slipping. A smart ass will tell you to shut up but will need some money or a ride later.

A relationship should be healthy not just dragging the shit out of someone else's dead weight because they look good, fuck good, or talk a good game to a person. Team work makes the dream work. A leech will kill you eventually. A person who won't grind will steal. A person who won't listen will end up in the hospital because when you were told to get down, you want to know what's going on instead of just following orders, and then you end up getting shot. Now this couple has to spend time at the ER because this bitch can't take orders from her first line of defense.

Letting the Defense Know the Plays

People get the word "team" fucked up. In teams, the word "my" is immediately out the vocab. No time to be a lil stingy ho, that what-is-mine-is-mine and what-is-yours-is-ours type stuff. Teamwork makes the dream work. All that I-do-what-I want-to-do mentality will get your ass kicked off the team really quick because you don't want to run the plays we practice. We agreed you boxout, rebound and pass the ball. You come down the court shooting like you Steph Curry. You can't just run your own plays. At the end of the day, you signed up for the shit, not anybody else. So, during this game of relationship, it is a must you understand it is two against all and family does count. For some reason, we think family needs to know everything but when we fucking. Everyone has the ability to destroy the team: don't dismiss anybody.

All relationships have a disagreement every now and then. That shit is normal. After a disagreement or misunderstanding, the first thing most sucker ass niggas do is go and tell the defense. We have to stop snitching on ourselves. Social media doesn't need to know about what the fuck is going on in your relationship. You should never expose the negative shit going on in your relationship to social media or any of that chatty-patty shit. You should really make people wonder what's going on. Make people miss you, not get tired of seeing you before they even see you in person. The main BAN in your crowd of media fans fucked up anyway cheering you on with the likes and comments. They are feeding off that negative bullshit you're putting out there. That's why they're agreeing with you, all the while just wanting more. These BANs like to call it the tea, the spill, the whatever you want to call it: there are certain things you don't need to be letting known about your relationship. Motherfuckers are always looking for something to gossip about. BANs be happy your ass looking silly exposing your weaknesses so willingly. BANs will turn around and use the weaknesses you just exposed against you.

You told social media, friends, and the family that Bae don't do this or Bae don't do that. Yo' lil ain't-shit snitching ass went and told the world, a.k.a the enemy, that your team's lacking. Now, what do you think is coming behind your silly ass rant?

Most bitches be all in their feelings, reaching for help, being an attention-seeking hoe, when you should just really be trying to find understanding with your partner. A BAN loves to start coming into your life to start shit because they're miserable, so you have to be careful who you surround yourself with and share shit with. A BAN can't stand to see a good healthy couple. So, when your bitch ass goes on social media running your mouth and letting social media know you don't suck that mushroom tip or eat that vajayjay, another BAN goes rushing and sliding in the DM ready to take care of Bae's needs because your selfish ass is not. All of sudden, other BANs smell problems and see a chance to destroy your weak-ass relationship, and now you all hot and bothered because you advertised your bullshit on social media and got the reaction that you wanted. These BANs come in reckless like you recklessly invited, and now you have an issue with that. Let's start thinking about what we advertise on social media or just say silent period.

Whatever attention you're looking for is out there, just let it be for your best gain. Don't let it destroy what you have, which is happiness. Everything can be going good for a year or however straight. One fuck up, you post it, now all of sudden you stamped fuck up too. Now when you start back posting love memes and those perfect couple pics again, BANs remind you of that time you fucked up. They normally don't let that go even if it doesn't concern them. BANs don't give a damn about shit not having anything to do with them because they don't have shit else to do but boo you from the stands all day long. They come out of nowhere, swatting your paper basketball shot in the garbage. They feed off negative bullshit no matter where it comes from. Once you post some shit on social media, it is on there. And BANs eat that shit for food.

BANs don't ever let you forget about negative shit because that is all they know: they breath that shit. So, when you do get your head back straight on your shoulder from exposing the weaknesses of your relationship and decide to get back on track, a BAN will still attack at the weaknesses your dumb ass gave out to them in the first place. Now, you're in your feelings because these BANs will not let you forget about the past or some shit that was fully understood between y'all and y'all have moved on from it. Why the fuck will you air out your own dirty laundry, like WTF? Social media should be social not personal.

Family members are the worst ones to snitch to, unless you are getting that ass beat. Then that is the time to scream for help. Other than that, keep your motherfucking mouth closed when it comes to negative shit going in your relationship. We have to stop running to family all the time when we feel things are not going right our relationship. Go to Bae who you seem to have the issues with. Most of the time, the issues be a misunderstanding. It could be they really not knowing their actions are making you feel a certain way. Be a real teammate and tell your partner what the fuck is annoying you instead of telling your lonely ass friend. Most of the time, eight out of ten of your family members will ride and only decide with you.

When Bae is doing good shit, you don't run tell family every little good thing Bae do. If you're not going to tell it all, don't tell it at all. The person you normally talk to or seek advice from is usually single and lonely. Of course, they will not put up with the shit you bitching about because they don't have anybody's shit to put up with.

Lonely BANs as friends will destroy your shit. They look at your relationship as in it taking away time you can be doing shit for them or with them. So, you have to be careful talking down about Bae, painting a bad picture of Bae to friends and family; then when Bae come around friends and family, Bae is getting treated with the low respect level you have placed him in mentally with your family and friends. Bae doesn't know that your two-faced ass been running your mouth about shit that doesn't include them, which led to them not getting the hospitality that is normally offered at meet and greet. You have to sit back and look at things and realize it is your fault if this happens. Now family and friends saying and doing slick shit to make Bae feel uncomfortable. Shit can pop off and lead to violence between family and Bae for no reason. Family can get killed or locked up behind your silly shit, and you still going to be fucking around with the same person when it's all said and done because you're not going anywhere.

Once you plant seeds of negative shit to the other side about Bae, it's kind of hard to justify how Bae is good to you or for you. Most things can be resolved if you just take the time to express how you really feel about what is bothering you with the person you have an issue with or feeling some type of way about. At the end of the day, take that shit to that person. When you're at work and have issues with the environment you work in, you don't complain to family or friends unless you just like to bitch about everything. You normally take your issue to the company you work for to seek change or understanding.

Everyone has issues at some point, so stop being scared to express what's on your mind. There should be nothing you can't tell or ask your partner. Your partner should be the one who you run to first. When it comes time to express yourself, first put your emotions in your pocket. Then, have a purpose along with some cause and effect to the feeling you are about to express. It helps your partner see what you're expressing easier without being so vicious. Holding shit back or being scared to express yourself is some weak shit. Give your partner one hundred percent of yourself to make your bond strong where no one can break it but y'all. In order to win this game, partners have to help and call out each other. If you must say anything about your boo, it only must be good shit.

Tripping Over the Shit That is Behind You

A relationship should be about growing and pushing forward in life. Everyone has a past and the past should stay in the past. Most of the time, it is best that you don't know the past because you can't change it anyway. People do grow up in life, and you never know the circumstances of people's situations they were in during that time. If you can't change the past, then why get mad about it or even hold onto that shit? What is done is done and can't be undone. Drilling someone about ex-lovers, past sexual activity, or choices that they made way before you came around is an automatic bitch move. You can't get mad for some shit back in the day. That is some bitch made type of shit. You are not Doc from *Back to the Future* or the young Thunder Cats. You don't understand the circumstances or mindset a person was in at the time before they met you. You don't have to ask all those 21 bullshit questions that you really don't want to hear the real answer to anyway.

We have to stop being worried about who, how, when and where someone did some shit. The reason BANs investigate shit like that is because they're insecure with themselves. A BAN worries about the competition and becomes judgmental instead of being happy being with you and worrying about what y'all are trying to build. It is better not to speak of the past unless something is hurting you and you feel it starting to spill over into the new relationship. Depending on the situation, keep the past to yourself.

BANs can't take knowing that their love has been plucked by someone they know or hang around. The family member or friend could be a BAN who wants to start some shit and be on some hating and lying shit. If there is no video or picture of any kind evidence, it is best to keep your mouth closed. However, if you feel like a BAN may try to start some drama, go ahead and put the shit out there so there won't be any misunderstandings or lies being told about what really happened. Time is all we have, so don't waste it where it is not needed. The wise always say take it to the grave.

When it come to your past, keep that shit to yourself. It's not anyone's business how many dicks you've sucked or how many bitches you've been with. A BAN can't take the truth. The truth will shatter a BAN's inside, and they will not, I repeat will not, get over it. A BAN has the tendency to keep bringing up the shit. Remember, a BAN is insecure, so the inside knowledge of what you have done, with whom, and how will just keep running through their minds like a replay. BANs are comparing and imagining as if they were a fly on the wall during your extracurricular activities.

Some BANs will continue to ask for more details about what happened during your extracurricular activities for a mental stroke so they can hold you accountable for whatever you say. It is like talking to the police. You have the right to remain silent because anything you say can and will be used against you in the court of love. It is like *yea I'm your friend until you say the wrong thing* in their eyes. Telling a BAN certain things like you had a threesome can fuck up your current relationship, especially if you are not into that anymore. Now you have a you-did-it-with-him-or-her-but-can't-do-it-with-me situation. As you can see, depending on whether your love one's heart is in the right place, unfolding secrets about your past life can alter or ruin a relationship. Just shut the fuck up about shit you did in high school or college. You didn't even know yourself. You were just experimenting like everyone should do before talking about being in a serious relationship. A disease is the only thing that needs to be brought to attention because that can be life-changing.

You can't let old shit go into a new relationship. A new relationship requires a new foundation. Nothing from your past bad luck of love seeds you attempted to grow should affect what you trying to grow now. All the bullshit you went through with other love seeds should be looked at as experience.

No one ever says it was my fault my love seed didn't grow. At the end of a relationship, whether it was from cheating, not enough time, bored, etc., very few people examine self or ask to see what was lacking on their part or what were they doing to cause the relationship to go down a dead end.

There probably was a time when you were everything you thought but still got treated like trash. Those are the times you were with a BAN trying to grow something. You can't help what you pick and try to help grow because sometimes good seeds and bad seeds look the same. You can only tell them apart after putting in a little time and paying attention to details. It is on you if you keep watering the same damn seed and nothing sprouts. Who is the fool—the seed or the planter—when, after a year of watering and TLC, no type of sprouting happens? Why even waste all that time ignoring the signs and playing? How many times do you have to keep paying or giving?

Sometimes, if you pay attention to details, you will get what you are looking for. Some people have to get slapped in the face with the picture to get the picture. Look through all the bullshit you've been through with the other seeds so you can learn what not to do the next time the opportunity presents itself.

However, it's not always that the seed is bad, naw, maybe it is you, BAN. Maybe it is in the way you are nourishing it. Every seed should be planted with the good faith that it will sprout with TLC. Don't start with the negativity from the past if you are actually trying to grow something.

It is normal to have a disagreement in a relationship. Two people that have feelings and different personalities will eventually have different views or ways of doing something. Adults learn to agree to disagree. Kids get mad and play the goofy ass I'm-not-talking-to-you game when shit don't go their way. We have to stop that silly shit. If you can't forgive or forget, there is no hope in your relationship. A person must be able to forgive someone for whatever harm was done to them. Everyone makes mistakes, but it is up to you to make the decision to forgive a person or not.

If you choose not to forgive a person, it is a must you cut them off period. Why stay around someone who just did you so wrong to the point you can't forgive them? It is natural if someone is doing you wrong for you to feel fucked up about it. At the time, there may be no understanding because we tend to get caught up in our feelings, ready to lash back with our inner bitchiness, but it is a must that we be able to control our emotions at all times. Our emotions will cloud our judgment every time. It is hard to see shit clearly when emotions get stirred up. Emotions are a powerful force. If you're not careful, they will make you jump off a bridge. Emotions can be as deadly as drugs because they can take over the mind and have you acting without thinking. This can lead to a dangerous situation if you're not careful. So, remember we must control our emotions at all times.

When shit happens in your life and relationship, think without your emotions and always assume innocence. Always assume that your loved one did not know what he was doing is wrong or harmful to you. Everybody don't use their common sense or have the same principles. You may see shit as clear-cut, but just assume innocence with these BANs because they weren't raised right. By assuming this way, it brings a good vibe to a situation and allows you to be understanding and able to read a motherfucker to see if they are full of shit. Be ready to be forgiving. Instead of giving a nigga 20 to life with no trial because you believe the BAN just knew better, please know that there are a lot of lost souls in the world that don't possess common sense. If this is someone that you really care about, always assume innocence.

If you forgive someone, forget about it and let it go. There's nothing worse than a BAN who won't let shit go. You can't change until you both are on the same page. Living life in a constant apologetic state is a game. BANs will try to make you feel guilty, to make their situation seem equal or less than something you did, or they just use that shit to get the things they wouldn't get on the normal basis. Fuck that! Once we turn the page, there's no going back. If a person can't forgive and forget, well the relationship is doomed. The reason I say that is because, if a BAN constantly reminds you of your fuck-ups, eventually the shit will get old, and that is unhealthy for a relationship.

Forgetting about what someone has done can be hard; but if you forgive someone, why keep bringing it up? Once you and your partner forgive or agree to disagree, learn how not to keep bringing the shit up. This is an important key to a healthy relationship. If you keep bringing it up, did you really forgive them? It may keep replaying in the back of your mind. Just don't speak on it or let it get you in your feelings every time that shit keep replaying in your head. Nobody deserves to deal with your crazy ass mood swings because your punk ass is in your feelings.

One of the worst things you can do is go to sleep mad. BANs will go to sleep in their feelings and wake up and go all out their way to replay those feelings in their head to create that same fucked up feeling. Why waste all that energy over some shit that could've gotten addressed when it happened? Going to bed with that don't-touch-me shit is for kids. Always address what is really on your mind and how you feel. Once you address the shit, hopefully then you can get some understanding. Nothing worse than being up late trying to solve a problem that could have been addressed earlier. You could have been fucking and sucking then some pillow tucking, and feeling good the next morning. Instead, you've been damn near arguing all night about shit a BAN been held in from last year.

What's Done Apart Can Rip Apart

The saying "what's done apart can rip apart" can be misleading because it seems as if you need to be glued to someone, but that is not the point. Everyone deserves a little me time. You're supposed to have different friends that you hang out with away from your partner. This way you can free up a little and relax your mind. Remember, a relationship is like a business. You need a break: you also can't just hang out with your fellow employees. However, it is a must that you not get distracted by doing your own shit so much that you are putting your partner on the back burner.

There are a lot of things which you don't need to ignore and should really pay attention to. Come from under that I'm-in-like spell. You become so happy just being in the presence of someone, you begin to forget your principles. A lot of things go wrong later on down the road because of that reason. All of a sudden, something a person does bothers you, but it was always there from the beginning. You just had on rose-colored glasses and didn't see it. Let's discuss an example of how what is done apart can rip apart a relationship if it is not managed properly. Assume a guy loves racing and has been racing ever since he was a kid. He is known for racing his car from time to time at the track. He has a woman, but she cares nothing about a damn race car. She just likes him. The guy always seems to take his ass down to the track, and that always is inconvenient with whatever plans she put together for them to do together.

People tend to let shit slide for a while, and then sooner or later, it will grow into a problem. She may start to think the track is his top priority in the relationship. You can look at this in different ways. *Should I really be with someone who loves things I hate? If I really like this person, should I really indulge in what he likes?* Let's say she starts going down to the track to see what is going on. It is damn near mandatory that she goes along to cheer or be his trophy. However, when she goes, she shouldn't make her presence unnecessarily known by being extra to the point that the spotlight is on her. She shouldn't go down there acting as if this is her day for racing. She should never take the spotlight off him. He needs to be able to remain focused on the race instead worrying about her crying about it being hot or bugs and shit.

If it comes to a time where he will not let you tag along, then some red flags need to be raised in your head. It may be that you just don't know how to chill and that fucks up the vibe; so, it may be best that you stay at home and hear about it later. Why be like that when you should be an adult and enjoy yourself and not let the inner BAN out? If he says only guys are allowed there, then respect that.

"Sausage party" is a man code violation. Dudes should never have a sausage party. "Sausage" means nothing but dicks, no bitches. A party full of dicks tends to lead to destruction, especially if liquor is involved. Boys just do stupid shit when women are not around. If you ever pay attention and notice that there are no women, violence starts because they have to be so-called hard and dare a nigga to look at them wrong. If your guy keeps saying he is going to a sausage party and you seem to keep getting left out you, you may want to watch him. You may not be the only one if you can't seem to tag along to any events.

Every man wants a trophy on his arm. We are competitive, and we like to show what we have accomplished. This is why we always bring up old ass high school sports stories…*I was this and I was that.*

If you are with someone, you should enjoy doing things to see them smile. Even if you don't like whatever it is they like, just because you care about them, you should be willing to do shit you don't like just to see them smile. If you or your mate don't feel that way about each other, the relationship won't last long. This is when that two-headed monster called jealousy comes in play. Nothing about jealousy has never been documented as good. That is why it is best to be with someone who enjoys the same passions in life. It is hard when you like something and they like something else and you have to choose what it is y'all will be doing because that means someone is going to get left out and feel they never get to do what it is they like. Even if you guys are not seeing eye-to-eye and you guys have plans, you should be willing to put aside the differences and go enjoy an event. No need to waste money because someone is in their damn feelings. A person never wants to spend money on a person who seems to be ungrateful. Once you have established that attitude, sooner or later you will find your ass left behind not going nowhere. Then you'll start complaining that y'all don't do anything anymore. I know you hear opposites attract, which may be true, but opposites also kill a relation if you are not being open and paying attention to details. There has to be balance in the relationship in order for it to work.

Happiness

Happiness is life. Happiness makes life worth living and gives you that drive to explore and smile and want to see others smile. Your goal in life should be wanting to give from a place of overflow. This means you are so happy that no one can make you happy, you make yourself happy, and they only can enhance it. That way you are never dependent on anyone to fulfill your happiness. You have so much happiness built up in you where you need to find someone to give some to. You start to give love or show love because you are filled with it and not worried about what somebody else is not doing. You are complete, your bucket is full, and this is a wonderful place of mind to be, because who do you really need?

Most of the time, in our mind, we don't get love in the same way that we give. Our minds don't mean shit in their mind: keep that in mind. Just because you will get up at 3 A.M. to get John from the side of the road, it doesn't mean John will come get your ass from side of the road at 3 A.M. You have to do shit without expecting things in return. If you never expect anything, how can you ever get let down from a person? When you have expectations, you're taking chances on other people making you unhappy. You never want to rely on anyone but self to make you happy, because only you know what you like and to what degree. Only you will go that extra mile for yourself.

The speed of the world today puts tough pressure on people to be happy. For some people, it comes too easily and it is the crew who just cannot seem to figure it out why they are not happy. Most of the time, it is the glasses you are looking out of. Sometimes, you just have to switch pairs. How are you looking at the glass?

Nobody should be responsible for making you happy. You should be making yourself happy. Life is about choices, and the great thing is you have the power to decide whether your choice will be good or bad and take in whatever feeling you want to endure. When a person feels bad, it is because you are telling yourself to feel bad, so your body will take on whatever the brain is telling the body to feel. This is the reason why you see crazy people hitting themselves and doing crazy shit to put their lives in danger. Crazy people tell their bodies to feel good from their dumb shit. The brain is very powerful, so be careful what you tell your body to feel.

The old saying "sticks and stones may break your bones but words will never hurt you" is a lie. Words do hurt you if you tell the body to hurt. Self-doubt starts to kick in if you choose to let it. Never let someone put their negative feelings on you.

Let's say you are leaving home headed to work on your normal route but construction is in progress so you have to make a detour. You made it to work with no free time before work as you normally do thanks to the detour. On the detour, you noticed a new ice cream place close to home. Now at this moment, you can curse your day before it starts, talking about you were almost late due to that construction or be excited about the ice cream shop you found that you can stop by on the way back home. If nothing physically hurts you, then fuck that shit when something interrupts your normal routine because your boring ass shouldn't be routine no damn way. Being routine may keep you in your comfort zone, but it brings no new excitement to your life.

Learn to create good feelings and make the best out of things that are not; and remember, just because you're supposed to assume something is bad as a society, does not mean you have to think that way. It is a must that you take control of your own happiness and always make time to investigate and get your own view.

Always stand up so that you will always stand out. It is not being cocky or assuming one is better. It is just choosing to take a path only a few seem to be taking. It is lonely but it feels better not to be a robot.

Being happy in a relationship can be challenging if you let it. A relationship is only what you make it to be. Remember, happiness comes from you. While in a relationship, you shouldn't look for your partner to make you happy. Your partner cannot read your mind nor should be able to dictate your happiness. Putting your life's remote control in someone else's hands is dangerous. Who in the fuck should have the ability to tell you to be mad or happy rather than yourself? No human should be like a god to you. Humans make mistakes, have feelings, and are not always going to have your best interests at hand. Be the controller of your own happiness, so if anything goes wrong, you can't blame anybody but your own damn self for it.

Your partner can enhance your happiness by adding things to your life. If someone is taking away from what you love, follow your mind or that little gut feeling that tells you to run and let go before it leads to a disaster.

It is a must that you prioritize your happiness. Always set aside time to see what self needs. If self ends up, down, and out, who can uplift you when you've been the one helping others. Watch out for those evil people who only show love to those who make them happy. Stay away from those types because they are like the fun police. Fun police are there to stop all fun unless they are involved in it or happy at the moment. Once their vibe is fucked up, they no longer want to see others happy, smiling, and enjoying their time. Avoid people who go tit for tat, those who only do what and as much as you do for them. People who keep count of shit they do for you are also ones to keep an eye on.

I have learned that people will rarely have the same heart as you. So, if you love big, the chances of getting it in return are slim. No one will live up to your expectations, so it is always best that you just love from a place where your love is an overflow, which means there is no room for anything but giving.

Happiness comes from what you see value in. Happy is just a viewpoint. You need to have the ability to see the good in everything rather than focusing on that tiny sprinkle of a flaw. If the negative outweighs the positive, then it is time to release the problem.

Whenever you have a problem, it is always your fault. If you learn to take responsibility for shit, it is much easier moving forward. No one else is to be blamed for your sad ass face.

Learn how to mind your damn business and stay in your lane. Worry about what is in front of you, and take life for what it is. As soon you start to get out of your lane, here comes the problem. Why is that, you ask? Because now you're in other people's lanes worrying about what the fuck they're doing when your shit is not straight. There is a saying: *sweep around your own front door before trying to sweep around mine.* Living a fucked-up life but worrying about somebody else's life is like going to work and not clocking in but worrying about somebody else not clocking in.

Not giving a fuck is an art. I found that the healthiest, happiest, and oldest people practice this art. It tends to let shit not get you down. Only when it comes to things like health or the kids must action be taken. The rest of the time, not giving a fuck frees you from a lot of stress. It has been said that there are two things in life: things that we can change and things that we can't change. Change what we can and fuck what we cannot. Most people drive themselves to an early grave about shit that they cannot change. No human can fly naturally, so why die trying to prove some shit that doesn't deserve the energy.

People do have feelings, so it is cool to have heart, but be careful because in these times, people are preying on the kindhearted. It seems that most people are just out for themselves. So, if you don't take care of self, who will? Does self really matter? That is a question that you have to ask yourself. You only get the respect that you ask or demand. People today will go out their way to say anything to make you feel as if your happiness means nothing if they are not happy. Stop trying to get validation from these sorry ass people who can't even uphold their own character that they are trying to portray. Be confident and courageous. Always take control of the situation and don't let it control you.

Knowing When to Shut the Fuck up

Niggas always feel the need to say something at times they really shouldn't. For some reason niggas always want to be heard, forcefully voicing their opinion when they really should shut the fuck up. People are so quick to talk just to talk, and more than half of that crew can't even understand the situation. People are so busy trying to put their two cents in that they can't focus on what is going on. Before even considering talking to someone, you have to talk with yourself. See if you really have any weight to what you are saying, and better than that, be ready for the backlash that comes with opening your mouth. Most people are not ready for that, but you have to be prepared to control the flow of everything and only talk about what you know so you don't sound like an idiot.

People that do the most talking are normally the weakest ones, always running that fucking flap. Weak people always have to explain themselves or feel the need to justify whatever they do; and as they do this, they watch for your reaction to see if it is affecting you. Through my years of watching people, I've learned that the weakest person always seems to make a move first, whether wrong or right. But you always need to be strong enough to take control of every situation. I have learned when asking for something or being in an uncomfortable situation, the plan always is to shut the fuck up, pay attention, and I will find out everything I need to know. If you just keep your damn mouth shut and listen, you will soon hear what makes a person feel a certain way.

In order to fill a need, you have to hear a want. You cannot force something on a person and it doesn't mean shit to them. Find out what the need or the want is by listening to what is coming out of the mouth or watching what is being done, and play off that want or that need. By play, I mean if I say I want a cheeseburger, don't talk about no damn corn on the cob, only stay with shit dealing with cheeseburgers like bacon or some shit to enhance it. You can't sell a person corn on the cob if they want a burger.

Whenever talking to someone and that person gets an itchy head, clears their throat, or something similar, these are signs of uneasiness. You can't sell a person something if you can't control them. If everything is on their terms, then it sounds like you're playing someone else's game. And we all know you can't win in someone else's game, so only play your game to increase the chance of winning.

If you are true and righteous, stay on your square and don't bulge. Always be willing to take your ball and go home. Never negotiate with terrorists, because once you start, it is a never-ending road. Try never to give the other person an option. Be straightforward and confident and believe in the shit you're talking about or selling. If someone asks you for a painting you just did and the sign said up to $650, immediately after asking for that $650, shut the fuck up. Let your opponent respond first. Always see if you get what you want first. You never know what you are dealing with. You have to make people believe, see, and feel the way you feel.

If you really feel as if you are deserving, then say it and feel as if you do. People can sense a lack of confidence.

After asking for $650 and your opponent shuts up and you immediately go down on price by facial expression or explaining in detail why it is $650, you start to lose creditability. You've given the opponent ammo against why you should not charge $650 or another option, which you should never do. You know niggas want to get a deal and feel like we won. That is why you jack it up then go down, because once you go down, you can't go up on price. Once we see it was cheaper, then we go crazy knowing you went up, and most of the time, we're not interested any more. If you can't get the $650, you say no deal and stick to it, or see how close you can get up it. Now let the opponent respond to see, if not $650, then what you can get out of them. Now you're about to see what you really can get and play your cards from there. If you start high, you can do nothing but go down on price. People hate to go up on price if they are on the paying side.

A good tool to use when negotiating a deal and somebody gives you a crazy offer is to ask what it is based on. Asking this gives you an insight on what the fuck is really going on in the brain of the person you're dealing with because these days people will get information from their three-year-old niece. You never know what people are thinking. Knowing what they are basing the price on gives you time and ammo to devalue their opinion and make sense of yours. If you go into an exotic dealership, their prices are not negotiable. You just can't go in there trying to make deals. It is understood that you get what you pay for. People go to a buy-here-pay-here lot to negotiate because we all know what you put down is really what the damn car is worth, so you go back and forth about price until both parties come to common ground. That exotic dealer is going to tell you to take it or leave it because it is true to what they stand behind.

You have to treat life the same way. Know what you stand behind. Be exotic. Don't negotiate with what you already feel about yourself. Don't be that buy-here-pay-here type going back and forth about your worth. If you don't want to pay the toll, then don't get your ass on the turnpike. Fake people always have to explain themselves because it is really not worth it, but they have to trick you into why it is a good deal.

There are sayings like "real recognize real" and "what is understood, doesn't have to be explained." People who don't know don't know because they don't know when to shut the fuck up. You can't learn if you don't listen, and you can't listen if you are talking. Unless you are teaching or being asked a question, shut the fuck up.

Never argue with a fool because he will drag you down to his level and beat you with experience every time. They can't argue by themselves. They may can talk, but never argue. Learn which battle to choose and always take charge when you do. The best way to get over shit is to take ownership and move the fuck on.

Verbal Contracts

Verbal contracts are very important to use in a relationship. They are damn near mandatory. They must be addressed early, because if they are not addressed early, it's kind of hard to hold someone accountable for something they know nothing of. Some things shouldn't have to be said, but BANs will act dumb, especially if it benefits them until you say something. Verbal contracts are the principles of the relationship. They are just understandings between people. Verbal contracts are rules and regulations during the relationship. Think of it more as a handbook to the journey of life you will be taking with them. You should never go through a relationship just assuming shit. You know we love to assume shit. In a relationship, there are plenty types of contracts you can make and should make. The quicker you imply the contracts, the better understanding and quality of a relationship you will have. If a person doesn't know that there is a no-phone-snooping policy, you can't get mad when they start snooping because they feel entitled.

I know you're thinking, *we're together and we shouldn't have anything to hide,* which is true. BANs do be doing the most, but you should keep your snooping ass on your own shit unless something just smack you in the face. Why be with someone who you can't trust? That is your fault if you're having trust issues. True enough, people may be in certain careers where they are around people a lot and can't help what comes with the job. Like police, nurses, and truck drivers are people who encounter different people on the regular and it comes with the job. Those jobs normally are the top cheater jobs.

The most important thing is always to know what you have and don't fool yourself. Don't start collecting a bag of flags. In sports, once a flag is shown or a whistle blown, there is a violation and a penalty. You don't just keep playing as if nothing happened. First violation, he or she should be fired just because he or she broke trust, but you run your business like you want to. I don't advise any contract breach to go unpunished only to be negotiated after some sort of violation. Even if you do find something because your bitch spider senses are tingling, ask yourself, "At what point in my life are you fucking up at?" Are you ignoring the signs, being a fool, not paying attention to details, or are you just being a BAN going through a person's shit like you're the damn police?

Opposite sex friendship is another major contract topic to bring up. There is nothing like understanding these parameters. The most preferred friendship requirement is same sex only. It just helps to keep confusion down. To each his own, but given the right time and place, when opposite sexes are involved, it is going down. What guy will say no to a good dick suck from a woman? I don't know any guy that just want to be friends with a female. We want to fuck. If we haven't yet, it's just because she has not given it up yet.

The time your ass needs to be at or leaving the damn house is a major contract topic for the BAN that think I-don't-have-no-damn-responsibilities-at-home. We're all grown, but unless you are working third shift at your job, I believe you need to leave before dark and have your ass back in before twelve because nothing but legs are open after that. A special occasion like family's in town or job-related activity going on can be understandable but be very clear and understand both sides. Some people think it's cool to be at the club when they have kids at home on school nights, then they're struggling to get them up in the morning.

Always get an understanding about who paying for shit. Nothing is free but an excuse, and it doesn't pay bills. Each household is different, but nobody should carry the weight by him or herself.

In a relationship, you will come across some crazy or self-diagnosed in-laws whose screws are not tight. You know those want-to-be-crazy until you get on some ass like somebody else in the family. Dealing with the in-laws can get crazy, so when having issues with live-wire in-laws, there is a special procedure that needs to take place. And the reason for the name "live-wire" is because, if you don't handle them carefully, they will blow up on you and will end everything. The best way to cool an issue is to let your mate handle it first to see if they can make sense out of the situation. This gives the family time to turn that light switch on in the head of that person. If your mate doesn't do shit after you just expressed an issue about their crazy ass kinfolk, well it is fair for you to straighten that ass out, but at least try not to whoop they ass too bad…just a two piece, no biscuit. By all means, though, try not to resort to violence, because your ass can come and go, but family here to stay whether wrong or right. So, if you can, just try to avoid fucking with them.

Stop bringing up that I-heard shit into your relationship. Fuck what you heard, bitch, what did you see? Better than that, what did you touch? Remember, it will be a lot of haters out there. These days, if you don't touch it, then it is not real, and what you are touching may not be what think you're touching.

That I-heard shit can be poisonous. We have ears for a reason. If you are not deaf, then get ready to hear a lot of shit. Believe in nothing you hear, and half of what you see. Some shit is just simple. Nobody ever had to tell you not to jump off a bridge. So, all that I-didn't-know shit only applies to specific shit, so specific that you know not to fuck her family member while staying at y'all crib. But make up your own guidelines that suit you the best. Every couple will be different, but damn near on the same foundation, just going through different phrases. It's just best to start up front on what you want and what you will or will not take, or soon as possible to hold each other accountable.

Assume Innocence

Assuming innocence is a good factor to live by plus it keeps the negativity down, which can lead to stress. You should always think the other person's intentions were good unless they are trying to fall on you with something sharp. There is a thin line between being stupid and assuming innocence. Your friend cannot keep getting put out and need a ride in the middle of the night every night for no reason. Sometimes, if shit don't sound right, then it's not right. Don't jump to conclusions: just pay attention to what is going on without wearing your feelings on your shoulder. Always pay attention to details.

Only control what you can control. Being insecure makes it hard to assume innocence, and a guilty conscience will run a soul tired. Being insecure is for these weak bitches who don't believe in themselves. To play this game of life, you have to have confidence and know your self-worth.

Assume you are a one of the best top 10 companies to work for in the world. Do you think they have an issue with employees playing around with their job, not showing up, bullshitting? The answer is no, because people who value their job show up faithfully because they know it is hard out here in the field. The people who take it for granted get fired. The boss doesn't say, "I don't want to start training over, so come on back." He will bring in a fresh set of legs who will be eager to work. Companies hate to keep hiring but refuse to let one silly ass employee fuck it up for everyone else. Big companies let you think you're getting away with shit to build a case on your dumbass, while you think they're being stupid so you keep doing stupid shit thinking you are just that fucking smart. One day you come in as usual, but they call you in the office. As you sit there in front of the big folks, they smile at you with the got-your-ass-now face and display all the evidence against you, so there is no going back and forward about this and that. It is just *bring my shit back and get the fuck off my property, go to jail, or just leave and don't come back* if they really like you and don't want to fuck up your life even if you don't care about it. They can see the bigger picture and just assume you didn't know better but should and need to learn through that lesson.

Being able to assume innocence, you have to be able to withstand a loss or go without. People who cannot go without or cannot handle sudden changes tend to panic when something's not going right. If you are a manager on duty with three employees with three specific jobs for each one, you just oversee that they are working. One employee does not show up as scheduled, which means you have to jump in a spot until Pat brings his ass in. A weak ass manager will be calling, thinking negative about Pat, assuming that he's out drinking and having fun since he just got that little check. A weak person thinks negative because his ass now has to work and he's only concerned that his funky ass has to put in some work now. A good manager will just call to check if everything is okay and see if he can do anything to help. If not, he let you handle your business and tell you to get that ass back to work as soon as possible because they need you and no one else is like you.

A guilty conscious always wants to put their shit on someone else. People know when they're not shit. That is why their conscious be driving them crazy and damn near will drive you crazy if you let it. You know how people can accuse you of something to the point you hear it so much, you believe it.

Don't let someone else dictate your life because you will be held accountable for it later; so be careful who you give your life's remote to.

Don't be stupid and let someone drain you to a slow death by killing your happiness. This is why you must protect your happiness and be slow to invest in unnecessary emotions.

We don't have to bark at everybody. Only be ready to bite when it is time.

It is sad to say, but a lot of love in today's society is like being stranded in the ocean with your partner where one can swim and one cannot. Does one love because what one can do for the other to help survive, or does one actually love the other genuinely? Normally, one will just tag along to keep getting that air until someone else comes to the rescue. If you don't watch it, a person can panic and take both of you out by only thinking of self. That is why you must know what you have, and don't ignore the warning signs.

Don't make the habit of picking up flags. Some people are hard to love. The people that are the hardest to love are the ones who need it the most. There are many people who didn't get the love they needed when they were younger. They'll look at you crazy when you show love. Most feel as if they are being set up or something. For example: one person grew up where any food in the house is for everyone to eat. If it is something you don't want to share, you better hide it. Another person grew up with the my-stuff-is-my-stuff-and-your-stuff-is-your-stuff rule, and it will be a fight if anyone touches it. Now when these two get together, it is like a yin-yang situation. One person always asking can I have some of your whatever and the response always the food is for the house. The reason for this is that person was raised where you had to get it in your own so that person moves and thinks differently, whereas person number one was shown love, knowing that we all are trying to make it.

The point I'm trying to make is everyone needs love. Everyone didn't get love growing up and don't get it now. You can tell from those two people in the previous example how two mindsets can be different. If you can't come from a place of understanding, life will be very difficult because then you will become judgmental or begin to blame others for things when you can just take responsibility for them yourself and move on. Assuming innocence helps with dealing with people with different mindsets because you never know what people have been through.

Assuming innocence is just having the ability to think positive about the negative thing a person can be doing and be able to understand what stance a person is coming from.

After that, be able to make a good decision without getting your feelings mixed in with the situation which can cloud your judgment. Everyone may be slow to your thinking, but not showing everyone that you know this is the key. It is like feeling sorry for their lacking and being aware of their ability. You can't get mad at a blind person for being blind. Either feel sorry for him or help him. When people don't know, they experiment. Just keep your eyes open and your mouth shut and pay attention to details, and everything else will take care itself.

Being Open-minded

You can enslave your own brain if you're not careful, and you can tell a lot of about others during this process. Being open-minded is kind of self-explanatory: it's all about being open to new things and getting out of your comfort zone. Very few people tend to get out of their comfort zone because few people like changes, but those who do will go farther in life. They realize that, in order to progress, there must be a change. I'm not saying all changes will be good, but I will say the same actions will produce the same results.

People who are open-minded tend to be more successful in life. They get a chance to experience the world in many different ways. It is crazy that most people never leave more than thirty miles outside their address unless it is for work, but be flexing and popping on social media or even around their little town like they are living this exotic life. Some people will only eat foods that they are familiar with and will not try any other food just because they think it doesn't look right, which is a silly way of thinking. Yes, many people are allergic to different things, and by all means don't play with your health, but if it's not for health reasons stopping you, step out and try something new. You may surprise yourself with how much you really like other cultures' foods.

Being open-minded is all about not judging a book by its cover, about not saying no before ever experiencing something. For example: if you say you don't eat seafood without having tasted it, that is some simpleminded shit. How dare you put a cap on your brain by saying that? There are so many types of fish and just so much other stuff out there that you may just fall in love, so don't limit yourself. How can you know what you don't like to eat if have yet to taste it? It is simpleminded to judge only by look, and you can tell the ones who do by looking at their partner. They date the same typical person that seems to fit the norm. They look good and are convenient. Even if it ends up not being good for you in the long run, it was just something quick to grab.

Ever hear the saying *don't knock it till you try it*? That saying will open doors to some of the most amazing things that life can offer. Instead though, your dumb ass sits around and goes to work and stop and get that $5 special and go home every day...nothing new. Every new year, you talk about your new resolution but still doing the same things. You barely leave the town you live in, let alone travel somewhere else. And do you even know what a passport is?

People who are close-minded are bored and boring. Those people tend to be by themselves as well. I say that because they do the same shit over and over and over again. Places they go eat, they don't need a menu, and the server already know them and what they want and how they want it. When you tend to be so predictable, then you may want to overlook your routine and start stepping outside the box. Do you and your partner only fuck face-to-face or play gymnastics all around the house with no holds barred unless one's health is at risk? Fucking face-to-face all the time will get you stepped out on after a while: you should have toys and all types of shit.

You should always want to fuel the brain with new shit. That is how you grow. Never put a cap on your thinking or let someone else put a cap on your thinking. You should thrive off trying new things. New things should be like air to the body and that is mandatory.

Being open-minded means you have to be grounded as well. What I mean by that is you can look for too much information and get lost. Too much information is just as dangerous as not enough. This also goes hand-in-hand with believing in anything somebody tell just because they look official. So, stay rooted while always testing what you believe in.

Always want to grow. Don't put a lid on your life. It is said true warriors always sharpen their swords. Your brain is your greatest weapon. Sharpen it daily with knowledge and keep it oiled with wisdom. This means you need to learn something new on the regular and not be routine.

Don't be a slave to your own thinking. Being a slave to your own thinking is like putting your brain in jail. During this process you are actually telling yourself to think, feel, and do certain things no other way which probably comes from popular demand telling you to do so. Freeing yourself from your own thinking allows you the ability to open up to people and to relate. There is nothing like being able to understand the way others think, feel, and do.

Never just attach yourself to one thing. Always be willing to find new, creative ways to enhance yourself. To be open-minded, you have to have nothing invested or no point to prove because you are willing to expose yourself to all kinds of possibilities. Being open-minded allows you to see all shades of colors instead of what closed-minded people see as just black and white. They can never relate, finding it difficult to understand different shit that may occur in life. This is why nobody goes to them for advice.

While keeping your mind open, you tend not to get let down as fast because you have the ability to see things other ways to make up for whatever may be lacking in a situation. It's always a person that can make a bad situation into a good one if you just give them a chance. Only few can do it because it takes someone who is true to themselves to be able to absorb it all. They have to be able to listen and see.

Shut the fuck up every once in a while. Stop acting as if you know everything. The day a person stops listening is the day that person starts to die because you can no longer receive information. If all you do is put out, what will be left after giving everything you got with no plan on receiving more in return? Even the highest of people tend to use open thinking because that's what makes them great communicators. Great communicators are great in being able to relax and free themselves of their own beliefs and experience the shoes of someone in a totally different position from theirs and still be able not to pass judgment and be able help.

Nobody likes being uncomfortable because it means you are not in control. You may not be able to control different situations, but you are always in control of your actions. Being able to control yourself is more than half the battle you face in life. Having the ability to be in a situation and take so many things from it can help you learn and grow. Not being caught up in your feelings left back in the past can help so much in a relationship. Not everyone has that control, but it is needed and necessary in order for a couple to withstand the bullshit that comes with life. You have to realize that they really don't hate what you're doing: they just hate that it is you.

Mind-fucking

It is amazing how much value we put on our cell phones. Almost everyone has a one, and that cell phone has to charge every so often. It is so bad that people will ask to borrow, or will even steal, your charger. People tend sit on the ground, hold their phone while standing, and even leave it in the corner or wherever an outlet is just to get a charge. We seem to make sure our phone is more charged up than our partner and wonder why Bae be acting funny, but as soon as that phone get to acting crazy, straight back to the store your ass is going. When Bae acts funny, you want to act slow, and let shit play out instead of treating your partner with even more concern than you would that damn cell phone.

Women can be challenging, or misunderstood, however you want to look at it. Women need affection. If you want your woman at her best, you must know that she needs affection. I do mean need and not want. Affection means to her just as much as that charger means to those electronics. A woman needs to be told how beautiful she is every day. She needs to hear that you love her, how much you miss her and can't wait to see her. A woman needs flowers, or some other token of love and appreciation, on the regular, not just Valentine's Day. Hold your woman's hand in public and make her feel special. When these BANs look, they don't have to guess: it is understood...*this is mine*. Open the door for her. Motivation to open the door is when she walks through, you get a clean shot of what her body really looks like without looking like a pervert. When you go out to eat, sit on the same side in the booth and keep her warm or play with each other or something. Send texts throughout the day about how much you love and miss her and cannot wait to get home to lick that beautiful face. Act like you just cannot get enough of her. Try to kiss and hug her 'til the point she be like, "Boy, get your ass back." Be glued to her every time she walks around. Let her know, "I just have to put my hands on that just because it is mine and I can."

I know most guys don't like listening to their woman's stories. Nine times out of ten the shit is not interesting or doesn't make sense to us, so we refuse to let our women vent, which she really needs to do. The best way to get by without getting hit or cursed for not listening is to massage her while she vents. Foot, back, neck, or hell, full body. If she is venting and she asks you something and you get busted for not listening, at least you're rubbing her feet and got distracted on them bunions.

You should always pamper her. You have to pay for your woman a pedicure if nothing else. Her feet should not look like yours. I'm not saying every week, but a treat every so often would be a nice gift. Pampering involves comforting, paying attention. Make handmade cards, don't always buy store-bought ones, or at least pick one that really says how you feel and not just grab the most convenient. Get some of your kids crayons and markers and draw some "I love you" hearts, xoxoxox, smiley faces with the tongue out which mean buffet style which means birthday sex. Buy a pack of construction paper with different colors for different occasions. If possible and your ass is not too lazy, mail them to her. Everyone is human so no one is perfect, but as long as you are putting the effort, that can basically fill 90% of her affection. Even though it will change next week. This shit is easy and practically free, if you know how to do it. Remember this shit is a must. If you don't charge her body, some no-good ass is ready to let her borrow his charger and so much more since you want to bullshit.

Enough on the ladies: it is time to charge the men up. Men are simple. You can make it hard if you want to. I'm going straight in. Men only need these three things to stay charged: sex, not hear about what happened to you, and praise.

First, sex—it is a must you suck his dick. Again, it is a must you suck his dick. And again, it is a must you suck some dick and shut the fuck up afterward.

Second, men don't really want to hear what happened at work today. He just listens so he can get some pussy later.

We know if we don't have time now, you will be tripping later, so we listen. I'll be honest, most women don't tell good stories. Some stories sound like Charlie Brown's teacher—a bunch of noise with no words. That's why we can't keep up with what you said. If men agree with something in the story, it's not because we're listening. In the back of our mind, we're thinking *finish please*, but we say yes to get you to continue the story and hurry up and get to the end. Most women will say you don't even know who Amber is during her story after she just asked you. You replied yes for the sake of conversation, but no she is going to hit you with you-don't-know-who-Amber-is and the conversation just went left due your little lie. So, for men's sake, try to tell as few stories as possible.

Back to sex because that is what drives us. Don't be his freak only on holidays and his birthday for you trifling hoes. Do you charge your phone only on holidays and birthdays? I doubt that you do. I know most of you bitches will say I don't have time, and I get that you may work full-time, go home and be full-time mom, cook and do homework, but at the end of the day, you have to make time to be the little dirty hoe that your man needs you to be. You can look can down on what you may call skanks, but you better believe your man wouldn't mind that lil skank.

BANs don't deserve anything but some work to do because they just sit at home being unproductive. When it comes to men, men handle their business. It is hard enough to fight the temptation that comes with being a good man. But you can do it.

Every real man loves to get his dick sucked. If he doesn't like to get his dick sucked, something is wrong with him. If you go down on him, and he says, "No, I'm ok. You don't have to do that," tell him to shut the fuck up. I find it weird that most guys won't let his old lady suck his dick but will throat fuck a hoe in the street.

Don't underestimate what giving good head and then leaving him alone for a second can do. See, while you leave him alone, trust and believe he is thinking about what he needs to do to get some more of that. When I say dick sucking, I mean some deep throat and gobbling, and noisemaking. Use your imagination. Look for videos if you need to. When sucking dick, he needs to hear sloppy noises not baby kisses like it is cute or something. Slop all over the dick and be nasty. No talking with your mouth full to stall time. If your jaws hurt, slow down. And remember, spitters are for quitters. Trust me, nothing should turn him off except back door action. Back door action is a surprise attack in any scenario and can get you hurt, so I don't recommend that at all.

There are 365 days/12 months in a year. Let's just say he gives a dollar toward your Christmas or anniversary gift every time you sucked or fucked him; would you be glad about your gift budget when it's time to go shopping? Would you be excited about your gift or would you end up going nowhere exotic, more like wally world where you can get your money worth? And how can you be mad at anyone but yourself?

A man gets up every day to take care of business. You should be so good to him that he doesn't even want to go work. You should be telling him what you're going to do when he gets home. If you're not into nudes, then send a picture with panties on a plate for dinner. Play with that pussy and get it wet, then walk by while he playing the game and rub it across his face and say, "Dinner's ready."

Bitches talk about what they go through. I feel you, but it is not all about you, hoe. Even though you go through shit, you find time to pick up that damn phone first thing in the morning instead of grabbing his dick and getting it popping. Instead, you want to see who's on and what's happening on social media. I'm not saying 365 fuck him and suck him. 2 to 3 times out of 7 days a week can change his and your life. Happy man, happy everybody. A happy woman means deals and a bunch of ultimatums.

Some of you bitches won't even hit the 20s if he calculated y'all's sex activity, and then you wonder why he hate coming home. Wondering why he sit in the car for 20 minutes before coming in the house. Wondering why he always stopping by other places before coming home. He's not coming straight home to your dusty ass because you're not sucking dick. Those bitches at the bar sucking dick for cheap while he paying bills, paying top dollar for your sorry ass who only wait for birthdays or when your ass want some.

The final thing is praise. Men love to get praised, to be talked highly of. Act as if he is your knight in shining armor. When he does something, like bring a bag of groceries home, praise him like you been starving for days. The next time, he will bring three or four bags in. Men like to feel as if you need them. They feel good knowing this.

People need to look at their relationship as a business that hires someone to do a job. When a person starts to be late, starts pulling those no-call no-shows, starts with the I-do-what-I-want-and-leave-when-I-want attitudes, it's time for them to be dismissed. You can do whatever if that's how you feel, but don't get mad when someone shows up to train in your position. A company will not let your silly ass run the company in the ground if you are not handling business properly. They will fire that ass and replace you. That is the same thing that needs to happen to your ass when you start to pull no-call no-shows during the relationship. If the first thing you do is pick up the phone, at least kiss your partner first, grab a dick or titty or something. Make your partner want to come home. Make them feel special, not tolerated, or they will go somewhere they are appreciated.

Making memories

When it is all said and done, memories are what most people rely on to get them through the rough times, because trust and believe, it will get rough. Having hard times comes with growing together. If you have siblings, hell you fought them every other day and was back playing with each other afterwards. You would dare a motherfucker to fuck with your family but fight them all day, and then laugh and talk about the times you fought or did stupid shit. Memories give you an opportunity for conversation and something to think about before you leave that ass. That is why you must plant good memories.

In a relationship, making memories is the key, so it important to try to make as many memories as you can. Go places and experience things. Try to have a lot of this-is-our-first-time type of shit when people ask you have y'all been here. As a man, it feels good to introduce his lady to some new shit even if he has not done it either. No matter what you go through, you will always remember the first time you did something together.

It is a must to have passports if you're not restricted. Go travel the world and experience what it is like outside the box you live in. Go eat shit you can't get back at home. A relationship bucket list is a good thing because it helps you set up a plan to do something new. Every year, take at least three trips, and it better be a damn good vacation. Try some all-inclusive resorts and get massages with full spa treatments. Let them scrap that husk off your feet while you sip a little something with a twist.

Remember, it is never too late to stop being a bitch ass nigga, and it is too late in the game to be one.

Made in the USA
Las Vegas, NV
30 November 2021

35703097R00085